FOREWORD

IT is a great pleasure to have been asked to write a foreword to Ted Carpenter's book. It reflects a good deal of research to have collected so many pictures, each of which has a story to tell, and many of which recall the situation as I found it when I came to Romney Marsh fifty-seven years ago.

Littlestone Road was then known as The Avenue, and graceful trees lined both sides of the road, with not a house in sight. On the beach dear Mr. Polhill had his bathing huts and many a young person owes his swimming prowess to his devoted instruction.

The old Priory at New Romney was then a private house and usually occupied by the local doctor.

One of the most remarkable changes of the last fifty years has taken place in the village of Dymchurch. From a quiet, sleepy village, it has become a flourishing popular sea-side resort.

Another peaceful village is St. Mary in the Marsh, although now it boasts a road, Rectory Road, of Council houses. What an untold blessing the coming of mains water was to these isolated Marsh villages, where the water was so brackish, from the wells. How vividly I remember going to tea at the Rectory and finding difficulty in hiding my distaste.

On the other hand Lydd is comparatively unchanged. The houses in the High Street look much as they must have done a hundred years ago when the Annual Fair was held in the High Street and there was dancing on the Plat in the evening. I must not forget to mention the noble 'Cathedral of the Marsh', as Lydd church is called. To see it as it is today reflects the heroic efforts made by the parishioners for eighteen years to ensure, after the devastation of 1940, that their church was restored to its former glory.

I congratulate Ted Carpenter on his book which will give immense pleasure to all lovers of Romney Marsh and far beyond the Kentish borders. Ted, born and bred in Lydd, has taken endless trouble to recapture the Marsh during the last hundred years. This is not only a worthwhile photographic record but also an invaluable portrait of the period.

Anne Roper

Littlestone
1984

Village Life

THE photographs record the closing years of the villages and small towns as self-contained communities. Romney Marsh has been luckier than many areas, the small towns have grown larger, while still retaining much of their original character. Most of the villages have at least one shop, one or two still have their schools, and villagers can still attend services at their local church, although at less frequent intervals than in the past. In all places there is still much of the old community spirit.

In the past the various town and parish councils, assisted by the local churches, played a leading part in the welfare of their local communities. Many in those days were poor — none were allowed to starve. The Friendly Societies, Foresters, Oddfellows, Enrolled, etc. were based on the public houses: they provided sick benefit and did much good work for charity.

In June, these, with the other clubs and organisations, held Hospital Sunday in Lydd and New Romney. All members attended church and afterwards organised a house to house collection for the local hospitals.

During the course of the summer the clubs and societies met once again, in their villages, for the annual Club Day festivities. These usually took the form of a procession during the morning, with band and banners, followed in the afternoon by a fair and carnival. There were the usual stalls and sideshows, with competitions and races for all ages. The tradition is continued in Lydd's Club Day, the others have now ended.

The church was instrumental in the founding of many village schools in the 1820s, including those of Lydd, New Romney and Brenzett. This work was completed by the Government under the Education Act of 1870, when every village had its school. The children in the photographs appear rather overawed by the occasion but their looks do credit to life in the Marsh. After the turn of the century many became members of the Scouts or Guides, represented, with the Boys' Brigade and Girls' Friendly Society, in towns and larger villages.

The majority of the adult population belonged to one, or more, of the local organisations. Many of them were keen supporters of their local cricket and football teams. Even Dungeness had a cricket pitch, especially laid on the beach near the Grand Redoubt.

There were clubs for those who preferred Bowls, Croquet, Quoits or Tennis. An ancient and energetic game, Goalrunning, was played by most local towns and villages. The rules are complicated and involve two teams of twenty-one men in a form of Cross-Tag. A similar game is still played on the other side of the Channel. As it seems unique to the coastal areas of both countries, the local story has it that Goalrunning was played before the Channel separated our two countries!

In the summer months, the sands of Dymchurch, Littlestone and Camber attracted locals as well as visitors. There were boat trips, donkey rides and sand castle competitions, the last sponsored by a chocolate company. If wet there were always the pictures, films were shown at Romney and Dymchurch before the first War. A barn was converted for use as a cinema in Lydd. This was replaced in 1916 by a purpose built cinema in the High Street. All have now gone, part of the yesterday of the older residents of Romney Marsh.

Above: The opening of the allotments at Lydd, c 1909. Each man had ten perch of ground to grow produce, to help supplement their incomes

Cottage Gardener's Society Autumn Show, c 1920. Being countrymen, there was keen rivalry in the towns and villages to see who could grow the best

A bevy of beauties on Queen Alexandra's 'Rose Day', 1930. Left to right: Alice Fisher, May Tart, Mrs. Waldron, A lady visitor, Miss White, May Tart's dog

The Southeast and Chatham Railway, St. John Ambulance team, from Lydd Station. They were winners of the Laurence Hardy Shield, 1911

The John Jones Coursing Club, taken in 1886, outside Eastbridge House, Eastbridge, Romney Marsh. John Jones is the gentleman on horseback

The Annual Club Dinner of the Friendly Societies. Many speeches and toasts were made, each society trying to outdo the other one. There was plenty of food and drink as well

A day down by the sea at Greatstone, c 1920.
The picnic basket strapped to the back of the cars.

Dymchurch Picture House stood by the bus station, later
becoming tea rooms. Built about 1913, it was open six nights
a week showing the silent movies. Photographed in 1920

The Thatched Barn at Lydd, 1910.
Once a Tithe Barn, this was converted to a Picturedrome
about 1908. Later on it became a Skating Rink, but was badly
damaged by fire in 1936

Relaxing at Littlestone.
Judging by the amount of clothes
on, it was not a particularly warm
day, Mr. Polhill's bathing huts
not getting a great deal of use.
The shrimp nets, ready for low
tide, lean against the huts.
c 1910

Children and their teachers of the village school, St. Mary in the Marsh. The Headmistress is carrying the cane, not for threatening the children, but more as a badge of office. Photograph about 1915

Pupils of Brenzett District School in 1908. All so well dressed, a credit to their school

Lydd School, showing the additional classroom built in 1898. The attached house on the left was occupied by the Headmaster

Dungeness School, with quarters for the staff, built about 1876. The first Headmistress was a Miss Richards

Brenzett School, erected in 1851 for 200 children. The photograph shows the children lining up for school c 1910

Lydd celebrates George V's Silver Jubilee with a procession through the town, 6th May 1935. A mixture of floats, motor and horse-drawn

The occasion of the visit to New Romney of the Duke of Kent in 1937. All the towns and villages sent representatives to New Romney for the occasion. The Mayor of New Romney, Major Max Teichman Derville on the left, Gordon Paine, Mayor of Lydd, centre

New Romney and Lydd Scouts in 1914. On the outbreak of World War One, the scout troops from these two places went regularly to Lydd Military Camp for training to assist the local defence in observing, and to act as messengers.
One of the scouts is carrying a gun, another a bow and arrow, perhaps a mark of their determination

Brenzett Club Day, June 8th, 1910.
A time when all the surrounding villages gathered together to enjoy the fun of the fair, the galloping horses, the roundabout, or to see who was the strongest and could ring the bell three times in a row

A village wedding at Brookland, the marriage of Mr. & Mrs. George Brann in June 1913.
Just the occasion for showing off those lovely wide brimmed summer hats decorated with flowers

New Romney Town Band, c 1910.
Very popular in the district, and always extremely well turned
out, they were invited to play at most Romney Marsh
functions

Lydd Town Orchestra, c. 1905
Concerts were held regularly in the town. The Orchestra used
to lead the Club Day Procession, which started from the
Rectory in Dennes Lane. They were criticised by the clergy in
1906 for playing music likely to corrupt the inhabitants of
Lydd. The music is unfortunately unknown.

New Romney Football Club 1912-13, taken outside the
Warren Inn. J. Taylor, C. G. C. Wolfern, P. Kennett, Taff
Jones, S. Harris, S. Lamacraft, A. W. Williamson, J. Harris,
C. Carey, F. Link, Ted Best, Stead, V. Oiller, W. Hooper

Lydd Goalrunning team outside the New Inn in South Street.
A fine bunch of extremely fit looking men: note the bare feet
— most teams ran barefoot. The liquid in the two jars is
naturally for medicinal purposes only. c 1912

'Trotty' Holdstock in training for the annual Mile Race on
Lydd Club Day. George Stredwick his trainer needed a bicycle
to keep up. Taken about 1915

Shops

THE photographs appear to have been taken over a period when shops and shopping had reached a pinnacle of convenience for those who lived in the small towns and villages of the Marsh. Even the smallest villages had at least one shop where daily necessities could be purchased. In the larger villages and small towns most trades were represented and deliveries to outlying areas were normal practice.

All butchers slaughtered their animals on or near their own premises. In New Romney there were two abbatoirs within a hundred yards of the school. Members of the older generation recall the squealing of the pigs competing with the voice of the teacher.

Bakers baked their own bread in brick ovens fired with wood. The grocer patted up butter and served sugar in cone shaped bags, made up in a moment from sheets of blue paper on the counter.

Milk was delivered from door to door, by producer-retailers carrying highly polished cans with the measures hung inside. These men, mostly small farmers, would also sell eggs and cream.

Both New Romney and Lydd had Chemist shops. Mr. C. Geering had the larger premises at Romney and was locally famous for his home-made cures, which ranged from foot powder to lung tonic. Mr. Greening at Lydd doubled as the local dentist; treatment was carried out in the garden, the patient being held in the chair whilst the chemist plied his forceps.

There are still plenty of shops in the small towns of the Marsh where service is as willing as ever.

In Brookland there is still a butcher who delivers over a wide area, although he no longer kills on the premises as his father did before him.

The village shop, alas, has almost gone, and with it the ha'penny sherbet dabs and the pen'orth of aniseed balls.

Above: Hughes' Butcher's Shop in Lydd, 1912. Inside the shop doorway is Mr. Hughes. The display of meat was a fairly common sight, especially at Christmas time. Today the local dogs would approve, but the Health Inspector might not

The Bakery, Corn Stores and Forge at Appledore, c 1890. Still an excellent Bakery and a well-known Forge. The Corn Stores is now a Craft Shop

White's General Store in Coronation Square, Lydd, c 1925, delivered to all the Coastguard Stations scattered around the coast by horse and cart. They were rivals to Hutchings' which was just across the Square

Smith's Garage and Store, 1905, in West Street, New Romney — rather a strange combination. Mr. Smith his STAR Motor with his wife in Car. The second car is a de Dion

Vye & Son, the Kentish Grocers, in West Street, New Romney, the same premises as occupied in 1905 by Smiths. Vye & Son became part of Liptons, which still has shops in Lydd and New Romney. Left to right — Manager Ron Capel, Les Martin, Charlie Gosling, Ray Holden, Doris (Bubbles) Jones, Eddie Piper

Blacklocks & Wellstead in the High Street, Lydd, c 1920. Motor Car, Motor Cycle and Bicycle agents; Rudge and BSA cycles stocked, Royal Enfield Motor Cycles, petrol and paraffin in one gallon cans

A small but very necessary shop, serving Ivychurch in the 1920s, was Mr. King's Grocery and General Stores and Post Office. Any order could be placed here — from a Sunday suit to a perambulator

Hutchings General Store, Lydd, c 1900, at the time the forerunner of today's superstore. The horse and cart delivered to outlying districts and the boy with the hand-cart did the local delivery in town

Jane Adams' small shop at Dungeness stood near the lighthouse. It sold tobacco, fruit and vegetables, confectionery and grocery items

Greening's Chemist's Shop at Lydd c 1930. There are advertisements on the wall for Cooper's Sheep Dip, Dogwash and Kodack films. As most Chemists were also the local photographers, some of the postcards on the wall, taken by Mr. Greening, are possibly included in this book

Public Houses

IN the first part of this century public houses played a more important role in the social life of the villages and small towns than perhaps they do today. They were the centre point for the inhabitants to meet, discuss and organize the village affairs, before the days of the village halls.

Most village fêtes, Club Days and sporting matches such as football, cricket or goalrunning, were generally arranged by the pubs, creating a great sense of rivalry. The Friendly Societies were also run from public houses — it was these benefit clubs who also collected regular subscriptions from members, to aid them should they fall sick. They also combined together to hold the Club Day dinner, celebrated afterwards with a march through the towns and villages, with their banners.

Another need for the pub was for the workmen (in the early part of this century few women would be seen in such places) as a place to relax and discuss their work, or even to find work by being in the hub of things.

Wedding receptions and even Coroner's Inquests have been held in such premises.

As in other coastal districts, these establishments on the Marsh have been associated with the smuggling trade. The George Inn at Lydd was the scene of a battle between Revenue Officers and Smugglers. The Old Billy at Camber, the Woolpack at Brookland, the New Inn at New Romney and the Ocean at Dymchurch all abound with stories, true or not, about the smuggling trade.

A number of publicans also supplemented their income by hiring out saddle horses or by private stabling. Mr. Moody of the Victoria Hotel in New Romney was an Omnibus Proprietor.

Eighteen of the Public Houses on the Marsh were owned by Edwin Finn & Sons, Brewers of Lydd. Edwin Finn first began in 1862, and in 1878 he bought the brewery in High Street Lydd from Alfred White, and six Public Houses.

In June 1892 a dinner was held for the staff of Edwin Finn & Sons to celebrate the completion of their new Brewery in High Street, Lydd. On October 19th 1921 the Brewery, with 40 public houses and five off-licences, was auctioned in London.

To compare prices, it was 7 shillings for $4\frac{1}{4}$ gallons of strong ale, 4 shillings and sixpence for bitter ale and 6 shillings and sixpence for London Stout in the year 1901. One must, however, bear in mind that wages were a lot lower than they are at the present day.

Above: The interior of the Royal Oak, Brookland, taken about 1910 — not a can of beer to be seen. Plenty of bottles of Farmer's Ale, Finn's Pale Ale, recalled by the 'oldens' as Real Beer

Park Street, Lydd, showing the Royal Mail owned by Beer & Rigden; it was the only inn in the town which was not owned by Finn House Brewers. Photographed in the 1930s

At the entrance to Dymchurch stands the very old established inn The Victoria, now renamed The Ocean. In 1921 the landlady, Mrs. C. Swift, had been the occupant for 45 years. The houses on the left have now been demolished

Another pub, the Woolpack of Brookland, is said to have been associated with smugglers. In 1890, when this photograph was taken, the Woolpack was kept by the Brignall family, whose ancestors certainly were smugglers. The Brewer's Dray is Eagles of Hastings. One of the most popular pubs on the Romney Marsh

On the crossroads at Brenzett still stands the Fleur-de-Lis. A peaceful scene in 1910, when horses were the only traffic. Now the A259 passes within feet of the door

Affectionately referred to as the Old Billy, the Royal William at Camber, 1900, later destroyed by fire. It stood in the sand dunes by the Golf Club House on the Rye side of Camber. It was said to have been a meeting place for Smugglers

Victoria Hotel, New Romney, c 1900. The proprietor was James Moody (seen with the dog). He also ran the stables from here and an Omnibus to Folkestone and Lydd Station. This was also the Posting House

Pope's Hotel, Littlestone, was the largest Hotel on the Romney Marsh. It was originally called The Grand Hotel and was built for Mr. H. T. Tubbs in the 1890s. Many public figures came to stay here in the years before the First World War, to play on the nearby Golf Course

The Dolphin Hotel, newly painted, stands on the corner of the Rype at Lydd. Photograph taken August 1911. The proprietor Mr. W. Brown and his wife stand in the doorway. The brick wall on the end encloses the gentlemen's toilet

The Rose and Crown, Old Romney. Hardly recognisable today — the photograph was taken in 1928 when the pub had sawdust on the floor and a spittoon in each bar

The Alliance Inn, Brookland, was an Edwin Finn house, and in 1910 had three bars, a coach house and stabling for 3 horses. Today is has altered little and stands beside the A259 Rye Road

The laying of the single track road from Boulderwall Farm to Dungeness in 1925, part of a scheme by Lydd Council for the unemployed in those difficult years

Pope and Bakers Waller gangs rebuilding the sea walls. Skips towed by horses were loaded by hand, the clay dug from some nearby area. These earth walls have in recent years held the sea back after the main sea walls have been breached

Employment

IN the years before World War II the chief sources of employment on Romney Marsh were farming and fishing. Although these industries are still important the numbers of jobs available, especially in farming, have greatly decreased. As large employers of labour their place has been taken by the power stations at Dungeness.

Edwin Finn's Brewery in Lydd employed a large staff drawn from the town and surrounding districts to produce his Kentish Ales and Aerated Waters. Another large employer was the Lydd Military Camp which drew men from Lydd, New Romney and Brookland.

The exploitation of the large beach deposits by quarrying companies employed a number of local men, and still continues to do so. Civil works such as the construction of the lighthouse, the many coastguard stations, the water towers, the laying of gas and mainswater, the construction of better roads, all these throughout the years helped to provide employment.

The protection of the Marsh from the sea and the drainage of its land have always been priority tasks. Horses towing skips of clay to build sea-walls, and men equipped with wooden spades and ditching trugs, have been largely replaced by machines, steel and concrete.

The rates we pay now apparently originated as early as 1250 in Romney Marsh to pay for the repairs to the sea wall.

A Beach Quarry on the New Romney to Lydd Road, c 1925. The Crusher is driven by this old steam engine, with the beach being wheel-barrowed up onto the Crusher

Granger Dickens with his men in July 1906 at Lydd, laying the mains water to Manor Road. The two small cottages were taken down in the 1930s

Some of the men laying the Main Water to Lydd from the Waterworks at Dungeness. They have just reached Cockles Bridge on the Dungeness Road

The bicycle enabled men to travel further afield to seek work, and to see or hear large groups of cyclists in the early morning on the road to work was not unusual in the years before the Second World War.
Lydd men at Church Road, New Romney, c 1910

A more unpleasant job, but still very necessary, was the clearing of the Dykes, to allow the surface water to flow out to the sea. A very cold and mucky task with long narrow spades and trugs

The staff of Finn's Brewery, photographed in December 1907, to mark the occasion of the owner Alderman Edwin Finn's 20th year as Major of Lydd (centre, with the black bowler on)

The Churches

THE churches of Romney Marsh have a fame which extends far beyond their immediate area. Each one has unique features which commend it to the visitor. Probably the sparseness of the population and the remoteness of the Marsh spared most of the churches from the attention of Victorian restorers.

Over the years, since the photographs were taken, income and Church attendance have declined and the fabric of the buildings has suffered. This process is now being arrested by the activities of the Romney Marsh Historic Churches Trust, a body deserving of support.

The height of the tower and length of its nave have conferred upon All Saints', Lydd its title of 'Cathedral of the Marsh', although the people of Ivychurch also lay claim to this distinction. Lydd Church, the oldest on the Marsh, was badly damaged by enemy action in 1940 and was restored after the war at great cost, two thirds of the money being raised by the people of this small town.

At St. Nicholas, New Romney, the ground level of the church is the former level of the surrounding land. Around 1287 a great storm forced the River Rother, which until then had reached the sea at Romney, to find a new outlet at Rye. The town of New Romney was covered by several feet of silt which was cleared from the Church but was allowed to remain in the street, thus accounting for the discrepancy in ground levels.

Although of Norman foundation, St. Peter and St. Paul, at Dymchurch, is one of the few local churches to have been extensively altered. Much of the nave was rebuilt in the early years of the last century to accommodate an increasing population.

Inland lie the churches of the Marsh villages. All have their points of interest and it would be unfair to compare one with another. Perhaps St. Clement's, Old Romney vies with St. Thomas Becket at Fairfield as the most photographed. St. Augustine's at Brookland is the most frequently visited, its detached belfry and rare lead front being but two of its attractions.

The visitor may wish to see E. Nesbit's grave at St. Mary in the Marsh, and to see Snargate Church, where the Rector was once Richard Harris Barham, author of the *Ingoldsby Legends*.

The Churches of Romney Marsh are certainly worth seeing and saving.

Above: St. Mary-in-the-Marsh, c 1920. As the name suggests, it is a church in the Marsh, just a few houses and the Inn clustered round it. It is of Norman origin, but Saxon records suggest evidence of an earlier church here

The Parish Church of St. Peter and St. Paul, Dymchurch, 1936. Traces of Norman work can still be seen after the major structural work carried out in 1821

Known as the 'Daffodil' church, for its beautiful yellow display of this flower in spring, St. Augustine at Snave is seen here in c 1920 in better times, a small church in a smaller hamlet. It is now being rescued from the brink of decay by the Romney Marsh Historic Churches Trust

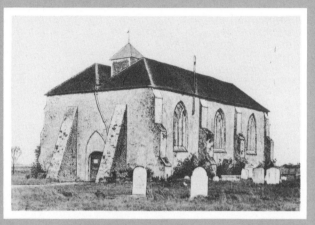

The Parish Church of St. Mary, East Guldeford was built in 1505 by Sir Richard Guldeford and stands on the Level of East Guldeford, just in East Sussex

A fine view from the old school gardens of the Norman Church of St. Nicholas, New Romney, 1910. The 100 ft tower is built in five stages and said to be one of the finest examples of Norman architecture to be seen

St. Augustine, the Parish Church of Brookland, is the most visited church on the Marsh. Photographed in 1915: the small shop on the right, belonging to the Bottle family, was demolished about 1953 for road widening

One of the earliest photographs taken of St. George, Ivychurch in 1874. The photograph shows no signs of neglect and decay which, it is said, was the case around this period. The picture shows the small spire on the turret, the chimney on the north wall, and the 3rd window from the right (an example of the decorated style) none of which features are still extant, probably having disappeared in the major rebuild of 1903

At one time ivy covered, the Church of St. Peter and St. Paul at Appledore photographed in 1900. The present church was built in the 13th century, possibly on the site of an earlier one

An early photograph of Lydd Church, taken in 1880, clearly illustrates the height and length of this 'Cathedral of the Marsh'

On the 15th October 1940 a bomb-carrying Messerschmitt 109 fighter dived out of low cloud, made for the church, and scored a direct hit with its bomb in the chancel. Such is the excellent quality of the restoration work that visitors today may be forgiven for not realising the devastation which occurred in 1940

It is not surprising that the small Church of Fairfield, dedicated to St. Thomas Becket, had to be rebuilt in 1912 due mainly to rising damp, for most years it was surrounded by water. The first photograph shows it in 1890 before restoration. The second photograph shows reconstruction taking place in 1912-13, the materials sometimes in 1912 being ferried to the site because of flooding

Fairfield Church shown after the rebuilding, in flood in 1921. The fenced causeway was built in 1913. This area was extensively drained in the 1960s making this scene a thing of the past

Lydd Volunteer Fire Brigade

LYDD Brigade was formed in 1890 because of several fires which had occurred in the Romney Marsh district. Until then fire cover in the Marsh had been supplied by Rye, Tenterden and Ashford, all some considerable distance away. A meeting resulted in the Lydd Council building a fire station and purchasing a twenty-two man manual fire appliance from Merryweather of London. Captain Harold Finn, of Lydd, would command the Brigade, New Romney was under District Fireman J. C. Moody, Brookland and Brenzett under George Capeline.

The manual arrived in August 1890 and in the following week it was publicly tested with satisfactory results. The hose was carried up the steeple of Lydd Church to a height of between seventy and eighty feet and a jet of water was thrown from the nozzle to a height of another sixty-five feet. This was extremely good bearing in mind that this was a hand pump appliance.

On April 5th, 1913 a new Shand Mason was purchased, paid for by public subscription, and the Merryweather became reserve engine. Both of these engines were horse-drawn vehicles, but in the late twenties the steamer was towed to fires by the local Brewery Lorry.

The Shand Mason, which had given good service, was sold in 1930 and replaced by a motor fire engine made by Dennis Motors. This was purchased second-hand from the London City Fire Brigade, again by contributions and donations. It had solid tyres, so the men certainly had to hang on tightly on the rough roads, but it enabled a better and faster cover of Romney Marsh.

The fourth engine was bought in 1940 by Lydd Council, a new fast appliance, again by Dennis Motors.

Although the Volunteer Brigade had considerable success in fighting fires, it was their results in the National Fire Brigade Union competition that brought them fame. City Brigades, as well as volunteers, entered these competitions, but Lydd Brigade won the Challenge Shield on several occasions as well as other Trophies.

In 1891 a young man named Herbert Blacklocks joined the Lydd team and by 1895 was undisputed 'All England Champion', a title he held for a considerable number of years.

Lydd was invited to many European countries where they won certificates, diplomas and medals. They took their Merryweather Engine to Paris to an exhibition in 1900 to give demonstrations and were well received.

The 1890 Merryweather Manual Engine has been restored and is now being kept in Lydd's Museum.

Above: One of the biggest fires the Brigade had to deal with, on the 6th September, 1928, was Smithers barn fire. The engines of both Ashford and Hythe also attended this fire

The last Fire Engine of the Volunteer Brigade, made by
Dennis Motors in 1940. Lydd, like all brigades, was
incorporated into the National Fire Service

The first 'Dennis' engine, purchased from the City of London
Fire Brigade in 1930 enabled better and faster coverage of
Romney Marsh and the surrounding districts.
Left to right: Back row — R. Wellstead, S. Boulden, A.
Balcomb, T. Wellstead, H. Terry (Captain). Front row — B.
Browning, T. Prior, B. Mittell, F. Cole, F. Austin (Driver)

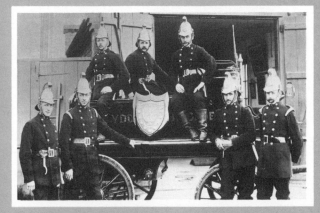

The team who won the District Challenge Shield for the six
man drill, which they won four times.
Left to right: Back row — Engineer G. Munds, H. L. Cole,
H. Allen. Front row — C. Cole, Lieut. Bishop,
H. J. Blacklocks, Capt. H. Finn

The Shand Mason Steam Fire Engine towed by the local
Brewery lorry, off to the barn fire at Eastern Road, Lydd,
1928

Mr. H. J. Blacklocks competing at Margate in 1895 in the
one-man drill tournament. He went on to win a record time of
sixty-one seconds

The day after the fire at Godfrey's barn, which was
completely destroyed on the 1st May 1909, despite gallant
efforts by Lydd Fire Brigade.
In 1974 fire also destroyed the thatched barn in the
background

Gobles Smock Mill, flames being fanned by a strong westerly
wind. This mill caught fire whilst being dismantled on the
22nd September 1927

Fireman H. J. Blacklocks,
the 'All England
Champion' of the one
man drill competitions. He
went on to become Captain
of the Lydd Fire Brigade

Towns and Villages

ROMNEY Marsh is the collective name for the district which, in fact, consists of three marshes in Kent — Romney, Walland and Denge, with Guldeford Level just over the border in Sussex. Romney Marsh proper covers almost half the total area, lying to the north of the Rhee and Appledore Walls, now the line of the Romney-Appledore road.

This part of the marsh has been inhabited since pre-Roman times and its settlements are of great antiquity. The largest of these is New Romney, one of the original five Cinque Ports but now stranded a mile from the sea. Until 1287 the River Rother reached the sea at Romney, its estuary forming the entrance to the port. In that year the last of a series of violent storms caused the river to change its course to a new outlet at Rye. The loss of the river caused the silting of the estuary and the decline of the port. Despite the passing of the years and the many changes, New Romney remains a busy and prosperous town, still retaining many of its old and interesting buildings.

The coastal village of Dymchurch is now part of the almost continuous development which has taken place between Hythe and Dungeness over the past fifty years. The once quiet little village is now a thriving small seaside resort, very busy throughout the summer months.

The inland villages remain much as they were, although there has been some recent development. Newchurch is typical of most, with a Church, Inn and Village Shop and a nucleus of houses with a scattering of outlying farms and cottages.

With the exception of Brenzett all the village schools have closed.

Until the early Middle Ages, Walland and Denge Marshes consisted of a shingle bank and sand bars, interspersed with creeks and mud flats. Settlements took place wherever a sufficiently dry area of shingle or sand existed. The marshy land was gradually reclaimed, chiefly by the monks of Canterbury.

The town of Lydd stands upon one of these ancient beach banks, and evidence of an early settlement here is given in a Saxon Charter of 740 AD. During the twelfth and thirteenth centuries Lydd grew in importance, eventually becoming a Limb of the Cinque Ports.

Lydd, despite the modern developments of two Nuclear Power Stations and an Airport, is still a much quieter town compared with its neighbour Romney. There has been some post-war housing development, but it retains its old world charm and its streets and buildings continue to bear comparison to the early photographs.

Other villages in Walland Marsh vary in size from the largest, Brookland, with its rural dignity, to the small hamlets of Fairfield and Midley.

Fast growing Camber is just in Sussex — another seaside place with large extending sands drawing numerous tourists every year.

Above: New Romney High Street — 1920.
A 15 lb German Gun, a prize of the First World War, stands outside the Post Office, but was taken away in the Second World War to make armaments for our country.
The house with the lamp hanging outside was the Wesleyan Chapel and House (upon this site today stands the Methodist Church).
Parked outside Mr. Kirklands Chemist (formerly C. Geerings), is a two-seater car.
This photograph certainly depicts a much quieter scene than the busy High Street of today

An early photograph of New Romney taken in 1890: Alfred Bates' Butcher's Shop is now the Electricity Showrooms. The village pump can be seen further down on the same side. Because of unmade roads, there is a Lady's walk, a brick path across the side roads, to help keep the long dresses clean

New Romney High Street, c 1900.
The horse and cart coming up the street belonged to Mr. S. J. Wiles, father of Mr. Jackie Wiles — later Mayor of New Romney. Mr. Wiles was a high class butcher, and used to deliver from his shop in Newchurch on Tuesdays and Fridays. On the right is the town pump, and further down on the same side is the Town Hall, and the New Inn.
The first shop on the left was for many years the premises of Ashdown & Sons, Saddle, Collar & Harness Manufacturers, Established 1770

Ashford Road, New Romney. This peaceful scene in 1900 with the children playing in the street, the stone walls of the 13th century Priory showing clearly on the left. This is a curious place even today, with its grotesque open-mouthed Corbel-Head staring down on passers-by. On the left the open door of Neames Bakery, and then the shop, at one time the Rose & Crown. In the background appears the Norman Tower of St. Nicholas Church

The bridge at Appledore over the Military Canal, called the Gateway to Romney Marsh. In the 1920s boats could be hired from here for the day, and one could row as far as Iden Lock, or Warehorne in the opposite direction

Appledore is still a small attractive village, with many visitors in the summer. Scenes as rural as this have long gone, however. c 1936

The Avenue (now called Littlestone Road) c 1910. This road takes one to the sea front. Today most of the trees have gone, and houses line the road, spoiling one of New Romney's natural attractions

Another way to enter the Marsh is through the village of Hamstreet, shown here in 1900, with Mr. Joy looking out from his forge. The wagons outside the old Duke's Head are carrying kettlenet poles destined for the coast

Littlestone Convalescent Home.
Designed by Percy B. Tubbs, FRIBA, and established in 1905 by Louise Elisabeth Tubbs and her sister Mrs. Clara Mary White with financial help from their father Henry Thomas Tubbs, who had been Mayor of New Romney, as a Convalescent Home for patients suffering from post operative debility. Private individuals and Companies could subscribe and send a patient there for one guinea for two weeks. The South East and Chatham Railway gave cheap rail fares from London

Brookland looking towards Brenzett, c 1920.
Apart from the small building on the left, the street has changed very little today. It is still a pleasant village, and apart from the traffic, it has retained a lot of its character

The Grand Parade, Littlestone, built in the late 1880s for Mr. H. T. Tubbs as holiday homes for the more affluent society. The drinking fountain commemorates the Diamond Jubilee of Queen Victoria, 1897. Photograph c 1920

A desolate scene at Dungeness, before 1925 — a small track to the lighthouse, which the present road is now laid upon. The lighthouse and the base of the previous one, the signal station, the first world war fort, coastguard and fishermen's houses made up this remote settlement

A view from the fort, built about 1750.
It stands at the entrance to Dungeness, looking out onto the small houses of the fishermen, which are within easy running distance of the No. 1 Lifeboat Station, seen in the centre

The Lydd to Camber Road in 1925. How small the road looks compared with the present day. You can no longer drive up on the left side road to the sands

This end cottage was lived in by Mary Banks Tart and her husband Richard, both infamous smugglers. both are buried in the nearby churchyard, Lydd. The cottage has now been demolished. Photograph 1905

The only remaining thatched cottage in Lydd today. It stands on the edge of the Rype, and is called Grisbrook Farm. This photograph was taken c 1885, before the road was built in front

A rather heavy and late fall of snow occurred throughout the Marsh on the 3rd April 1909, as the photograph illustrates. Many lambs were lost in this year, through being frozen to the ground

The centre of Lydd, 1910, now called Coronation Square, commemorating Edward VII, formerly called Wheelers Green, and towered over by Lydd Church.
Many band concerts were given here on Sunday nights, with the whole town turning out to watch

Lydd High Street in 1911.
Of the two Marsh towns, Lydd has changed the least, retaining many of its old houses. Those on the right still look the same today

Viewed from the Church — Lydd High Street in 1900. Most of the buildings can be identified with the present, except the tall building behind the shops on the right. This was Edwin Finn's brewery, demolished in the early sixties

Butler's Shop and Post Office, standing beside All Saints' Church, Lydd. The gates to the churchyard were to keep the sheep out as they roamed throughout the town and its surrounding area

An early photograph of Lydd, taken c 1881.
The small building attached to the Guildhall was the lock-up, used to hold prisoners until trial. Many smugglers were held here, including George Walker, who made his escape in 1819, only to be killed by the Revenue two streets away

*Entrance to Dymchurch from New Romney, c 1910.
The Butcher's shop still trades, now under the name of
Hambrook. The weather-boarded house is now shops. The
tall building, once Smith's shop, is now a bingo hall, and the
small cottages are tea rooms*

*Same scene as previous but in the late 1930s.
Hambrooks are now the Butchers. Smith's stores have been
enlarged, and the roads have improved for the motorcar*

*The centre of Dymchurch about 1925. The tea rooms, on the right, were formerly the cinema. The bus station has
been rebuilt, as have most of the buildings on the left (note the old char-a-banc)*

*Since the 1920s Dymchurch has become the holiday centre of
the Marsh, and quite rightly so, with its long safe sands — a
paradise for children. An aerial view in the 1930s*

*Dymchurch c 1920.
The narrow road on the left is now the A259 to Folkestone.
The other road leads up onto the sea wall. The end building in
the centre was bombed during the Second World War and has
now been replaced*

Farming

BEFORE the outbreak of World War II Romney Marsh was predominantly a pastoral region, the home of the Kent or Romney Marsh sheep. As winter approached all young sheep were sent away from the exposed pastures of the Marsh to the high land in Kent and adjoining counties. When the grasses began to grow in spring the sheep were returned, the wethers for fattening, the ewe tegs to joins the breeding flock. If more sheep were required to control the exuberance of grass they were bought in at one or other of the local fairs.

In the Marsh shepherds are 'lookers', for in earlier days they were paid per head of sheep, some men working for two or three flock owners.

Most of the larger Marsh farms had some arable land producing corn, beans, roots and potatoes. The district was well known for seed crop production, especially turnip and wild white clover. The horse was the source of power, and the wagoner would attend to his team from before dawn until he 'racked up' in the late evening.

Over the period covered by the photographs the steam traction engine had become increasingly important as an alternative to the horse. Large farms often had a pair of engines which hauled a multi-farrow plough back and forth, from one to the other, across the arable. A single engine provided the power to drive the threshing drum, a task in barn and stackyard for the winter months.

All villages had at least one blacksmith, his forge being one of the centres of village life. Children and idlers gathered before the open door as the smith attended to the needs of horse and man.

Most places also had a windmill which ground the local corn. These became less busy as improved roads concentrated flour production in larger centres, such as Ashford. The last mill in the Marsh, at Lydd, was destroyed by fire in 1927.

Above: A large shearing gang at work near Dymchurch about 1890. A windbreak was a must on these windswept marshes.
Seven men hand shearing, two woolwinding, the old chap passing the cup, a mature 'lock boy', general assistant, the farmer in the centre with his two children, the boy holding the marking iron

Haymaking near Snargate, 1920, all the family turning out to give a hand. The Lurcher dog seen with the boy would hopefully provide a rabbit for dinner

*Newton's Steam Engines at Brookland, 1920.
Several farmers kept steam engines for hiring out, for threshing and ploughing*

*The threshing tackle at work, c 1920.
Every man had his task, the engine driver was usually the ganger, two men to feed the threshing drum, a man to take off the corn, the man with the buckets of water for the engine — and the postman liked his photograph taken*

A reaper at work near Brenzett about 1925. The sweeps (sails) pushed the corn towards the cutting bar, the sheaves were then bound and discharged, ready for stooking

A Ram Sale of 'Romneys' at Ashford in 1936. One of the oldest breeds of sheep in Britain

A Smockmill at New Romney which stood by Southlands School, Dymchurch Road. This Mill worked three pairs of stones.
Owned at one time by a Mr. Ashby, then later by a Mr. Carey. It was dismantled in 1914. The photograph is taken in 1901, showing it in working order

A sheep shearing scene on the Marsh.
The boy would bring the sheep to the shearers, mark the sheep and generally assist the shearers. c 1930

The founder members of the Romney Marsh Sheepdog Society. The proud mother showing her offspring, c 1936

Jack Pierce, looker to Merricks Bros., at Brookland, seen here tending the first born, c 1939.
The neck crook was used by the Marsh lookers, whereas others used the leg crook

Sheep being driven through the High Street of Tenterden, 1925.
A sheep fair was held annually at Tenterden and sheep could be seen being driven down all roads leading to it

Frank Cole's Forge at Lydd, c 1910. There has been a forge at Lydd on this site since 1801, founded by Thomas Cole. The last blacksmith George Cole (second from the right) sold it in 1959. Today this forge is a small museum and is combined with the Doctor's surgery

A "Sussex" bullock, brought from Ashford Fatstock Show for slaughter at Christmas 1900. This was then held by Mr. Hughes, Butcher at Lydd

A lady proudly displays a neat piece of shearing, using the old hand turn shearing machine, the young girl being the willing turner c 1915

Ted Paine with his workmen lifting parsnips at Lydd. The Royal Garrison Artillery man was probably buying the produce for his regiment. Photographed about 1912

Transport

BEFORE 1920 the speed of the traffic was determined by the gait of the horse. The roads in the Marsh were typical of most country districts, narrow and twisting, dusty in summer, muddy in winter. What public transport services there were, were horse-drawn. In the winter months an extra pair of horses was made available if the going became too difficult.

A bus or carrier service called at most places in the Marsh at least twice during the week. Mr. Moody of New Romney ran a service to Folkestone, starting from New Romney Station at 8.45 am on Tuesday, Thursday and Saturday. The horse-drawn omnibus called at Dymchurch, Hythe and Sandgate, and arrived in Folkestone at 11.15 am. The return journey started at 3.30 pm. The cost of the round trip was three shillings. This service was taken over by Carey Bros. in 1920.

A similar service from Lydd carried passengers to Rye and Ashford. Originally owned by W. H. Brown, the service was later acquired and run by Mr. George Allen.

A carrier service was of great importance to people living in country areas; Mr. F. Turk, of Lydd, ran such a service to Ashford on market days, collecting small items for sale and executing small commissions in the town. A similar service was run from Brenzett to Ashford and Rye by Mr. C. D. Smith.

Local deliveries to Dungeness, which in earlier years was not served by a paved road, were carried across the shingle in a light cart with wide wheels.

Towards the end of the twenties more and more cars were seen. Local tradesmen replaced their horses with motor vans; the char-a-bancs of the London and South East Motor Company were increasingly seen at Dymchurch bringing day trippers to the sands; one or two enterprising local firms bought ex-service lorries and used them for excursions to local events or sporting fixtures.

The rail link from Ashford to the Marsh was laid in 1881 — the establishment of the Military Camp at Lydd may have been a factor in its construction, for the transport of men must have been a profitable business; the standard gauge line was increased by six miles in 1883 from Lydd Station to cover the whole of the military area. In the following year the line was extended from Lydd to New Romney. There were plans to continue to Hythe, but these came to nothing.

The small gauge line of the Romney, Hythe and Dymchurch Light Railway was built by Captain J. E. P. Howey in 1927. It covers fourteen miles from Hythe to Dungeness and gives enjoyment to many people over the holiday season.

Above: Carey's Horse Bus. About 1930. This bus ran a service from the Grand Hotel, Littlestone to the Town Hall, Folkestone on Tuesdays, Thursdays and Saturdays. Single fare 2 shillings: return fare 3 shillings. Ted Peters (driver), Mrs. Moody, Mrs. W. B. Smith, Mr. Clapp and Mr. D. Carey

W. Browne's brake leaving the Dolphin Hotel, Lydd, with members of a Friendly Society

George Baker delivering coal across Dungeness beach, using the wide wheeled cart. c 1936

One of the small traps used by the ladies for visiting or shopping. Most of the outlying farms had one of these, as they might have a small car today

Old Jack Ford, from Dungeness, who used to sell fish, making a delivery along Manor Road, Lydd. Taken outside Grisbrook Farm, the only thatched cottage now in Lydd

Allen's Horse Bus, Lydd, 1910.
Owned by George Allen of Lydd, used to meet the trains at Lydd Station, for passengers and parcels under a contract for South East and Chatham Railway.
This fine bus has been presented to Lydd and is in the process of being restored and will be on display to the public in the future.
The photograph shows the Bus outside the Paddock, Lydd. Mr. Justine Smith is the driver

The tub cart was used discreetly at night to empty the cess pits and was known in Lydd as the 'Lavender Waggon'. c 1912

Mr. C. D. Smith with his Bean Lorry.
As well as being a carrier, he also undertook Furniture
Removals, Coach Hire and was a Coalmerchant too

Wessex RGA unloading their horses at Lydd Station in 1910.
The army made full use of the railway for transporting their
equipment whilst at Lydd for training

Lydd Station, 1912.
The line from Ashford to Lydd was opened on the 7th
December 1882, and extended to New Romney in June 1884,
with a branch line to Dungeness. The photograph, which is
taken from the station bridge, shows the view towards New
Romney, with the trolley just outside the station

Camber Tramway ran from Monkbretton Bridge at Rye
(A259 crossing the Rother) to Camber Sands, along the North
Point Road. Rails can still be seen in this road. The Tramway
was discontinued in 1940

One of the Romney, Hythe and Dymchurch light railway
engines, dwarfed by the standard locomotive at Ashford
Railway Works, c 1930

Loading hay, which had been purchased by livery stables in
London. All trusses were cut by hay knife, so strong wrists
and sharp knives were needed for this job, 1910

Edwin Finn & Son's Brewer's Dray, outside the Royal Oak, Lydd, at the turn of the century.
In the driving seat is Mr. Frank Caspall, and the other drayman is Mr. Edwards. The barrels on the ground contain 'Finn's India Ale' brewed at the Lydd Brewery, costing 24 shillings for an 18 gallon Kil, or a pint of Mild for 3 halfpennies (old money).
Edwin Finn owned the majority of Public Houses on the Marsh, and deliveries were made by dray once a week

Finn's Dray, St. Mary's Camp, c 1920.
One of the first Motor Drays bought by Edwin Finn & Sons. Seen here delivering to Captain Alnatt's holiday camp at St. Mary's Bay. An early Daimler Lorry

Customers of the Star Inn, Lydd aboard a char-a-banc, bound for an outing to Eastbourne, c 1913. Standing outside is the landlady, a Mrs. Toddman

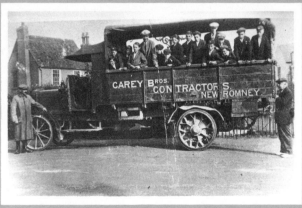

The Royal Garrison Artillery on their way to a shooting match at Hythe School of Musketry. Quite a load for two teams of horses over a distance of ten miles.
Photographed outside the Ship Inn, New Romney, 1912

An ex-service lorry used for conveying the public.
This must have been a very uncomfortable ride, with those tyres, c 1920

Royal Flying Corps

AN Aerodrome and Balloon School was established by the Royal Flying Corps at Dennes Lane, Lydd, about 1913. There were also two smaller airfields, one at Dymchurch, the other at St. Mary's Bay.

The first aeroplanes used at Lydd were the Maurice Farman MF7 Longhorn and Shorthorn. These were of French design with a Renault engine. The Royal Aircraft Factory's RE8 artillery spotter and reconnaissance machine was introduced in late 1916. This was an unreliable aircraft as the engine was prone to faults and landing was rather precarious. In 1917, although armed with one 303 inch Vickers gun and one Lewis gun, plus 224 lb of bombs, very many were lost in air battles over France.

A more successful plane was the BE2A, again made by the Royal Aircraft Factory, using a Renault V8 water cooled engine, a two-seater designed by the first Geoffrey de Havilland. This particular aeroplane was the first Royal Flying Corps machine to land in France during World War I.

A school for balloon training was also set up, shared between the Royal Flying Corps and the Royal Naval Air Service. The purpose of these large balloons and their crews was to register the fire of one gun on a certain target. When the observer saw the shell landing on the target he would then inform the Battery Commander, so that all of his guns could fix the range and presumably destroy it. These large balloons, attached to winch cables, were filled with hydrogen and underneath was suspended a basket in which the observers carried out their duties. In an emergency, such as being attacked by an enemy aircraft without sufficient warning to wind the balloons down to the ground, the observers, unlike the earlier army balloonists, could use their parachutes to drop to safety. There is no record of fatalities at Lydd during training on these balloons, although airmen were killed in crashes by aircraft. The reliability of these balloons during the First World War was high, a total of 407 parachute descents being recorded, and only eleven men lost their lives on balloon service.

The relationship between Lydd and the RFC was very good, they joined in the town's activities, held Christmas parties for local children and were noted for the annual 'Drome Concerts, which always guaranteed a large audience. They left Lydd for France in 1917 and apart from a few concrete foundations, one small hut and a few photographs, nothing remains.

Aeroplanes could occasionally be seen in the Marsh in the years before 1914. Several of the early pioneers of aviation made forced landings whilst en route from Croydon to Lympne aerodrome. A Mr. A. Ogilvie, who lived at Camber, was a familiar sight when landing and taking off from Camber Sands.

Above: View of Balloon Training Camp, 1915-1916. The balloon is of the 'Drachen' type, a French design, with the small basket slung underneath

Inset: Parachuting practice over Lydd, 1916. There were four balloons in training here with 100 personnel to each balloon

Mr. A. Ogilvie landing at Camber after his long distance flight of 147¼ miles on the 28th December 1910

A Maurice Farman MF7 ready for take off at Lydd: a box kite appearance, with engine at the rear.
In the background is Dering Farm

A Royal Flying Corps Officer in uniform — not unlike a Cavalry officer's dress, riding breeches, even a crop

A forced landing by an RE8 near West Brooke, Lydd. Unfortunately this type of aircraft was more often seen in these circumstances than in the air

After the departure for France in 1917 the aerodrome gradually fell into disrepair, as shown by this picture taken in 1920

A convoy of RFC lorries about to transport the Balloon School to France in 1917. The petrol winches are seen behind the fourth 'Leyland' lorry

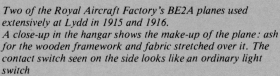

Two of the Royal Aircraft Factory's BE2A planes used extensively at Lydd in 1915 and 1916.
A close-up in the hangar shows the make-up of the plane: ash for the wooden framework and fabric stretched over it. The contact switch seen on the side looks like an ordinary light switch

Christmas dinner for the Balloon School's permanent staff, 1916. The message at the rear must have echoed throughout the armed services during that year

Army

ROMNEY Marsh has been used to the presence of the Army since the beginning of the French wars, at the end of the eighteenth century. At that time, with invasion feared imminent, the whole area was heavily garrisoned. With the coming of peace in the following century the Marsh was used for training.

In 1879 the first camp was established at Boulderwall, Dungeness.

A Major Fraser of the Royal Engineers conducted a series of musketry experiments carried out by the Scots Guards using the then new 'drop sight'.

In June 1880 two Batteries of Artillery camped at Boulderwall to fire a series of exmperimental shots. A large brick revetment was built between Dungeness and Dengemarsh and was used to test shell fire from eighteen and twenty-five pound guns and eight inch Howitzers.

All this led to the formation of a permanent Siege Artillery Camp at Holmstone, West Rype, Lydd — the present camp.

In 1881 the Royal Irish Rifles formed the first garrison of this camp.

The railway line was extended to the camp in 1883 for the use of the Royal Engineers who had erected workshops to service the whole area.

In 1906 the Royal Garrison Artillery carried out experiments with Box Kites and Balloons; this meant that the soldier had to ascend to about 100 ft in a basket suspended beneath the kite or balloon, to observe the fire from the artillery. These two methods of observation were not very successful since the men suffered from air sickness and had difficulty in controlling the balloons.

Most regiments of the British Army and also of the Commonwealth have stayed at Lydd. In 1924 the Camp became the permanent base of the 2nd Royal Tank Corps. In post-war years the REME had a base here for many years.

It is now an important training centre for all types of modern warfare.

Above: Preparing to fire a 9.45 Howitzer made by the Skoda works in Austria. These 9.45s were originally purchased for the South African war, to use if necessary against Pretoria

Royal Garrison Artillery Battery, practise firing a sixty pounder in 1912. The gun is well anchored to the ground because of the violent recoil

A Summer Camp on the Rype at Lydd, 1906, training teams of horses in towing guns and limbers. All Saints' Church Tower in the background.
The troops belong to 107 Siege Company Royal Garrison Artillery, under the command of Major J. G. E. Wynne

The Worcester Regiment arriving at Lydd Station Bridge after marching from Dover. One night's rest at Lydd under canvas, and then en route to march to Lewes in Sussex.
Photograph dated 1910

The 107 Siege Company Royal Garrison Artillery receiving instruction on their guns at Lydd, May 1911

Manhandling the guns along Station Road Lydd towards the camp, 1910. The troops arrived at Lydd Station and would spend two months gun training on the ranges

It is thought that one of the reasons for constructing the railway to the Marsh in 1881 was because of the military ranges at Lydd. In fact the army made good use of the rail service and a track was laid from Lydd Station to the Camp. Unloading a 4.7 gun at the Camp siding, 1912

The horse lines of the Garrison Artillery, 1909-10.
As many as 2,000 horses were tethered on the West Rype, Lydd during the periods of the Summer Camps. On the 6th August 1910, during a thunderstorm, 500 horses broke loose and bolted, seriously injuring one soldier and slightly injuring three others

The Army Farrier at work shoeing a horse of the Wessex Territorials of the Artillery, 1918

The Royal Garrison Artillery returning to the camp after attending the Sunday service at Lydd Church, 1911. The women and the children all in their Sunday best would usually follow the troops back to camp

The caption of this photograph, 'The arrival of the Berks., Lydd 1911', is a little suspect — they look more like Australians or New Zealanders by their hats and the casual way they are marching. I do not think a British Unit would have been permitted to do this

Towing the gun carriage through Lydd High Street towards the camp, passing New Hall and the George Hotel. 1911

The importance of the Railway to the Army is shown in this photograph. Horses and Troops are arriving on special trains from Salisbury Plain. The steam engine seen crossing the bridge is taking ballast from Lydd to Ashford

The 3rd Battalion Royal Tank Corps were stationed at Lydd from 1923 to 1938 and are seen here on Parade to Lydd Church during the Silver Jubilee celebrations of George V

Christmas Day in the Barrack Room of the Royal Military Police at Lydd, 1911

Royal Garrison Artillery carrying out their final work-up with eighteen pounders before going to France in 1915. These saw action on the Western Front

*Royal Tank Corps passing The Beehive, Lydd, in a Mark 2
Vickers Medium tank, first in service with rotating turret.
Photograph about 1930*

*Returning from Church Parade 1911, past the Royal Oak en
route across the Rype to the Camp. The young ladies were
hoping to catch a glimpse of their sweethearts — or perhaps
showing off their beautiful hats!*

*An earlier Vickers Tank which came off the rails of the
Camp Railway near Tarts Fishyards about 1924*

*107 Siege Company, Royal Garrison Artillery Tug of War
Team. Champions of Southern Command in 1903, 1904 and
1905. Trained by Major Wynne and C. S. M. Mursell*

*Lydd camp permanent staff were drawn from all Regiments
of the British Army. For relaxation they spent time
consuming the ales of E. Finn & Sons*

*These Kites and Balloons were used by the Army at Lydd for
observing the fall of shell on the practice range, 1906.
The batteries used six inch and 9.45" Howitzers, and an
Officer in the suspended basket telephoned details of fire to
the Range Officer on the ground. In good weather balloons
would be used, filled with Hydrogen, and in windy conditions
the kite would be used. The gentleman on the horse is
Colonel Samuel Franklin Cody, adviser to the British Army
on Kites and Balloons (often mistaken for William Cody
[Buffalo Bill])*

Guardians of the Coast

Lighthouses

ONE of the features of Romney Marsh is the great shingle foreland of Dungeness, stretching out into the English Channel. The Point extends seawards annually since it collects much shingle carried up channel on the tides.

Dungeness has been recognised as a hazard to shipping from early times. A lighthouse was certainly present in 1615; it is recorded that it was replaced in 1635 by a coal burning beacon raised on a 110′ platform. This rather crude structure was superseded by a new light in 1792; designed by Samuel Wyatt the new building was 116′ tall and consisted of seven storeys. The Wyatt light was damaged by lightning in 1821, but was repaired.

Trinity House built the next lighthouse, completed in 1904 it carried a pressurised paraffin lamp visible at a distance of seventeen miles.

The construction of the Nuclear Power Station obstructed the operation of this light which was replaced by a lighthouse of a modern design sited nearer to the point.

In addition to the tower lighthouses, Dungeness has had two low lights incorporating a foghorn, the first was built about 1880 and was followed around 1910 by a second. Both are now gone.

Coastguard

The other guardians of the coast are the members of HM Coastguard. Their predecessors were the Coast Blockade, raised in 1817 to deal with smuggling.

The Blockade was disbanded in 1831 and reformed as the Coastguard. The new force came under the jurisdiction of the Royal Navy, all ranks being required to spend a month each summer training with the Fleet.

Eleven coastguard stations were established on the Marsh coast between Hythe and the Sussex border. Each station had its own Watch House and adjacent quarters. All these buildings are now in private hands; only the Littlestone Watch House retains its original character.

In earlier days the coastguards manned the lifeboats and were involved in many rescues, some members of that service losing their own lives in helping to save others.

The modern Coastguard, although much reduced in numbers, still maintains its vigil on the coast.

Above: The staff who helped to build the 1904 lighthouse. Many of them were local craftsmen and labourers. The men in the hard hats would have been the tradesmen and clerks, the two on the extreme right of the front row are SE Railway station staff, and on the extreme left of this row is the Dungeness Postman!

The first of the low lights; necessary because of the shingle building up on the Dungeness Point, creating a greater distance between the main lighthouse and the sea

The second low light placed near the shore about 1909. These low lights also housed the foghorns and their awesome moan could be heard for miles in foggy weather

Because of the remoteness of the coastguard stations some form of transport had to be provided, so donkey carts were issued to all stations for collecting fuel and provisions from the towns and villages.
C. G. Wickenson & Family from the Dengemarsh Station, 1920

The 1904 lighthouse nearing completion. It was built by Patrick & Co. of London and is 136 ft tall and 38 ft in diameter. Close by is the 1792 light showing the base being converted into living quarters for the lighthouse staff. This is the white round house seen at Dungeness today

The Dymchurch Coastguard Station, built in 1905 on the site of an earlier station. In the centre is a Martello Tower built about 1802; this housed a patrol of the Coast Blockade in 1819 and was used by the Coastguards until the 1940s

Right:
A view looking down on the Jury's Gap station from the sea wall. In the late 1920s, as with the Dymchurch station, these replaced earlier houses. The block on the right was built in the 1870s and those on the left in 1897

Lifeboats

THE coast of Romney Marsh has always been notorious for wrecks, many ships and lives having been lost here over the years. The first lifeboat was brought about by the efforts of Captain William McCullock in 1826; it was stationed at Jesson (St. Mary's Bay) and crewed by the Coast Blockade. Dungeness Station opened in 1854, with an unnamed lifeboat. This craft was replaced by the 'Providence' in 1861, and this boat, after a few months, was moved to Littlestone where a new station was opened and the Dungeness one closed. This decision was reversed as a result of the collision at night, in 1873, between a large sailing vessel, the 'Northfleet', and a Spanish steamer the 'Murillo'. Many emigrants aboard the 'Northfleet' were drowned. In the following year, 1874, the Station re-opened with the 'David Hullett'. This lifeboat remained in service until 1887, saving twenty-seven lives.

Along the coast at Littlestone, a new lifeboat had arrived in 1871, the 'Doctor Hatton'. This in turn was replaced by the 'Sandal Magna' in 1884. During and attempted rescue on March 9th 1891 this boat capsized, there being a heavy sea running at the time and a raging blizzard; three of the crew were lost.

In the same year two other men were lost from the lifeboat 'RAOB' at Dungeness, this boat having replaced the 'David Hullett' four years earlier. An additional lifeboat was now added to the Station, the 'Thomas Simcox'. The second of two RAOB lifeboats was replaced by the 'Mary Theresa Boileau' in 1912. The last of the pulling and sailing boats, the 'David Barclay', arrived in 1915. This forty-two feet self-righter was launched seventeen times and saved fifteen lives.

There were two other boats at Littlestone over this period, the 'James Stevens' and the 'Harry Wright Russell'; the station closed in 1928.

Following the 'David Barclay' at Dungeness the first motor lifeboat arrived in 1933, she was the 'Charles Cooper Henderson', a busy and efficient boat instrumental in saving sixty-three lives during her service. Replaced by the 'Mabel E. Holland' in 1954, the 'Charles Cooper Henderson' went into reserve.

At the present time Dungeness is served by the Rother class lifeboat, the 'Alice Upjohn'.

The Littlestone station was re-opened in 1965 with an inshore inflatable Atlantic 21.

It is worth remembering that the early lifeboats, together with the Life Saving Rocket Apparatus on shore, were crewed mainly by the Coastguard.

Memorials in local churchyards and cemeteries testify to the number who gave their lives to save others.

Above: The crew of the Dungeness Lifeboat RAOB, the majority are coastguards, who gallantly manned the lifeboat until about 1906, when the task was taken on permanently by local fishermen.
They are members of the RAOB Hamlin Lodge, and the Buffalo Horn can be seen on top of the lifeboat

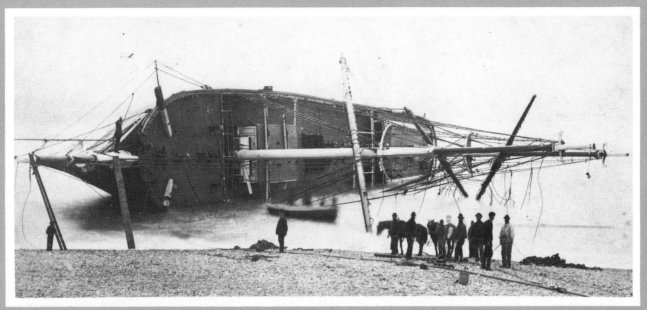

The Van Dieman in 1895 wrecked at Galloways in the West Bay. It first came ashore at Dungeness and while being towed off in a northerly gale, broke loose and was swept along the coast. The photograph shows men attempting to unload the cargo

Dungeness Crew c 1907.
An all local fisherman crew with the No. 1 Lifeboat, the 34 ft RAOB, the Coxswain still using a Cork Life Jacket

The women launchers have a proud record at Dungeness since 1895. These women carry on the proud tradition, pulling out the first motor lifeboat the 'Charles Cooper Henderson' which served at Dungeness from 1933 until 1957

Barque Schiller 1906.
The Barque Schiller of Bremen, Germany became stranded in rough seas off Littlestone on November 5th 1906. The Littlestone Lifeboat 'James Stevens' and the Dungeness Lifeboat No. 2 'Thomas Simcox' rescued the seventeen crewmen

Left:
Wreck of the Imperial Airways 'City of Ottawa' which came down in the sea off Dungeness on the 17th June 1929. Seven out of 13 people were killed

Fishing

THE rich fishing grounds off Dungeness have provided the local fishermen with their livelihood for many centuries.

One of the earliest Fisheries Protection vessels was stationed here in 1867 to prevent the poaching of fish stocks by French boats.

In earlier years, in addition to Dungeness and Rye, there were small fishing communities at Dymchurch, Littlestone, Dengemarsh, Galloways and the Brooks. At that time it was sailing boats and drift netting, from autumn to spring, for herring and sprats. Much of the herring catch was smoked in one or other of the local 'herring hangs' or smokehouses; Lydd kippers and bloaters were famous, there was even an export trade.

With the arrival of the petrol engine the small craft took to trawling, adopting the methods used by the larger vessels from Folkestone and Hastings. In high summer the mackerel was the main catch. Although numbers were taken by the boats many more were caught by Kettlenetting, a form of trapnet fishing which dates back on this coast to before the Middle Ages. The method used exploits the mackerel's habit of swimming along the coastline, close inshore in pursuit of whitebait. Stakes were driven into the sand at low tide and so arranged as to form a gradual lead into a circle. Nets were suspended from the stakes, and anchored at the bottom. When the tide rose, the patrolling shoals were gradually funnelled into the circular trap. As the tide receded, and the water level fell, men would either scoop the fish into a cart, or operate a small horse-drawn trawl net to tow the trapped fish ashore. Some mackerel were sold locally, but the majority were sent by rail to Billingsgate. The last Kettlenet was operated until 1953 by the Gillett family of Lydd.

Seine netting to catch inshore mackerel was sometimes used as an alternative to the Kettlenet. This method involved the use of a longnet, one end of which would be anchored firmly to the shore: upon the approach of a shoal, a small boat would be rowed out in a large circle, towing and paying out the net, against the tide. The net was kept upright by cork floats, the bottom was weighted with lead. When the shoal arrived within the barrier of the net the boat was rowed quickly ashore, closing the circle. The men then hauled the net and catch ashore — a method as old as time, as successful with running salmon as shoaling mackerel.

Above: The Rye fishing fleet at anchor in the River Rother at Rye Harbour, c 1910

Fishing smacks of Rye harbour leaving the Rother for the fishing grounds off Dungeness, c 1900.
The large sailing boats were used for trawling, which sometimes brought them into conflict with the driftnet men of Dungeness

Seine net fishing from Dungeness beach c 1900. Putting to sea with the net, one end would be anchored to the beach, and the net payed out around the shoal

After netting the mackerel, they are hauled ashore by the two groups of fishermen

Fishermen and their wives pose for the camera in c 1899, on the day of the Dungeness Regatta, started in 1895 by the Rev. Joseph Castle, curate of the coast

A good catch of Mackerel, being hauled onto the beach, near the Brooks, The Gillett Family c 1912

A good example of the Kettlenet, the range running from the beach, the round trap or bythe at the end. The men with the small catching net and the cart for bringing the Mackerel ashore — Brooks, Lydd 1912

The Gillett family pulling the fish ashore from the kettlenet, with a seine net. Some used this method to sort and load the catch

Loading the cart from the net using netted scoops and baskets. Patience was required from the horse